Sonny's Bridge

Jazz Legend Sonny Rollins
Finds His Groove

LIVING STEREO

THE BRIDGE
Sonny Rollins

LSP 2527   SIDE 1
(N2PY-1268)

1 – WITHOUT A SONG
(Youmans-Rose-Eliscu)
2 – WHERE ARE YOU
(McHugh-Adamson)
3 – JOHN S.
(S. Rollins)

STEREO

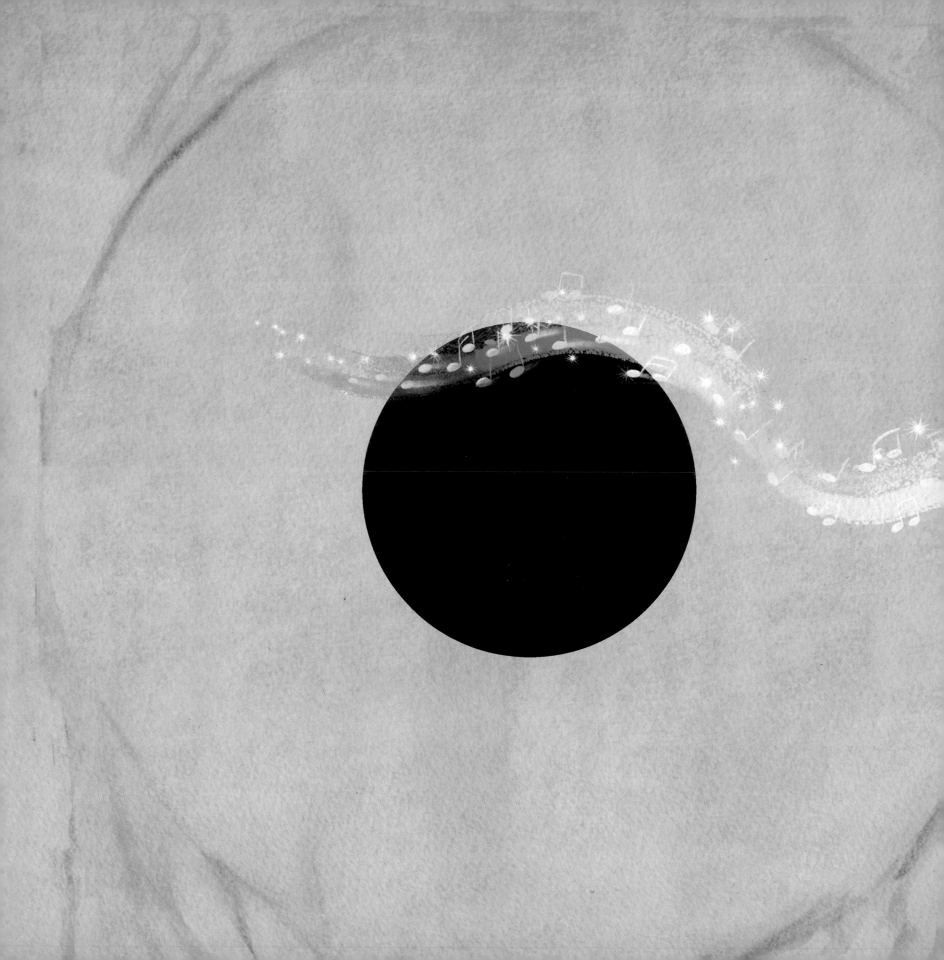

SONNY'S BRIDGE

Jazz Legend
Sonny Rollins
Finds His Groove

THE BRIDGE
Sonny Rollins

LIVING STEREO

LSP 2527

SIDE 1

STEREO

Barry Wittenstein

Illustrated by **Keith Mallett**

Charlesbridge

Misty night.

Summer night.

East River New York City night.

You hear that?

Hear what?

That. *THAT!*

Somebody's playing the saxophone. So what?

So that's Sonny Rollins, that's what.

Wait. *WHAT? That's* Sonny Rollins? *The* Sonny Rollins?

What the heck is Sonny Rollins doing on the Williamsburg Bridge

this time of night?

Nobody knows, man. Nobody knows. 'Cept Sonny, and

He. Ain't. Sayin'.

Born right place, right time.

137th Street, New York City.

Harlem Renaissance, 1930.

Sweet sounds of swing jazz swirl in the air.

Sir Duke's satin melodies.

(That's Duke Ellington, for you younger cats.)

Lady Ella singing scat!
(That's Ella Fitzgerald, if you didn't know that.)
Count Basie and Glenn Miller in the mood
with their jukebox and radio tunes.
But nothing beats stompin' at the Savoy–live!
The fox-trot, Lindy Hop, mambo, and jive.
Big band swing will never die.

Sonny shuffles his way to grade school.

Passes an eight-by-ten glossy in a jazz club window.

Louis Jordan looking dapper in tux and tails,

his golden King Zephyr sax ready to wail.

That's me, Sonny dreams. *That's me!*

THE DYNAMIC
★ ★ ★ ★ ★ ★
LOUIS JORDAN

IN PERSON

A few years go by . . . Sonny gets his very own horn.

First time he holds her in his arms,

falls in love—won't let her go.

Doesn't even hear his mama calling him for dinner.

He's blowing crazy in his bedroom closet with the

doors closed.

Nothing else matters. *Nothin'.*

World War II.

Soldiers overseas defending *de-moc-ra-cy*.

Return home, still fighting for freedom: their own.

A harder, faster sound scratching at the front door.

Together, a new generation of cats—

Charlie "Bird" Parker and John "Dizzy" Gillespie—

inventing a musical language nobody ever heard before.

Painting rhythms with colors nobody ever seen before.

Taking risks jazz musicians never took before.

This is the soundtrack in Sonny's ears

on the corners, stoops, and streets of Sugar Hill.

Its name is

BEBOP.

Sonny sneaks into the Apollo Theater on 125th,

the Cotton Club, and Minton's Playhouse.

Watching, listening, learning.

Nurtured under the wings of the jazz kings.

Turns nineteen in '49.

Giggin' around town 'round midnight.

People startin' to notice—Who's that kid on the horn?

He's nice! He's new! He's hot! He's cooooool!

Soon Sonny's becoming a **BEBOPPING** jazz king, too.

Turn the page to Rosa Parks, arrested 1950s.

Sonny plays fancy joints and two-bit joints.

Two shows a night, two sets per show.

Changing phrasing, evolving, *ex-per-i-ment-ing*.

Slowly building up *mo-men-tum*.

Then **BOOM BOP BEBOP!**

Hold on tight, 'cause Sonny explodes.

Im-pro-vi-sing at the speed of light.

Notes going places.

He doesn't even know where they're goin'.

Rockets to the top of the jazz universe.

His albums *Saxophone Colossus* and *Freedom Suite*

hailed as milestones.

Now headlining at 57th and 7th.

(That's Carnegie Hall, for you out-of-town cats.)

Awarded the jazz king's crown.

NEW YEAR'S EVE
JAZZ
AT
CARNEGIE HALL
SUN. ☐C. 31 · 8:30 P.M.

SONN☐
R☐LL☐S
& CO.

JOHN
COLTRANE

☐ ATTRACTIO☐
☐N☐A S☐
EXTRA !
☐EL☐US M☐
& BAND/

SAXOPHONE COLOSSUS

☐REED☐☐
SUITE

But it's too heavy, Sonny says. *I'm not ready.*

Ain't that just like Sonny!

Can't stop looking for that

One. Lost. Chord.

Question: How much greater can a great become?

Sonny's answer: *I'll tell you when I get there.*

HARD BOP, SURPRISE, STOP!

Twenty-nine in '59, in his prime,

Sonny shatters the jazz world.

Throws up his hands, lays down his horn.

Looks in the mirror,

doesn't like what he sees.

Name bigger than talent.

That's some hard truth to swallow.

Jazz scene like an A train, speeding

in the wrong direction.

Sonny knows if he don't jump,

He. Won't. Last.

Rumors circulating: maybe Sonny's never coming back.

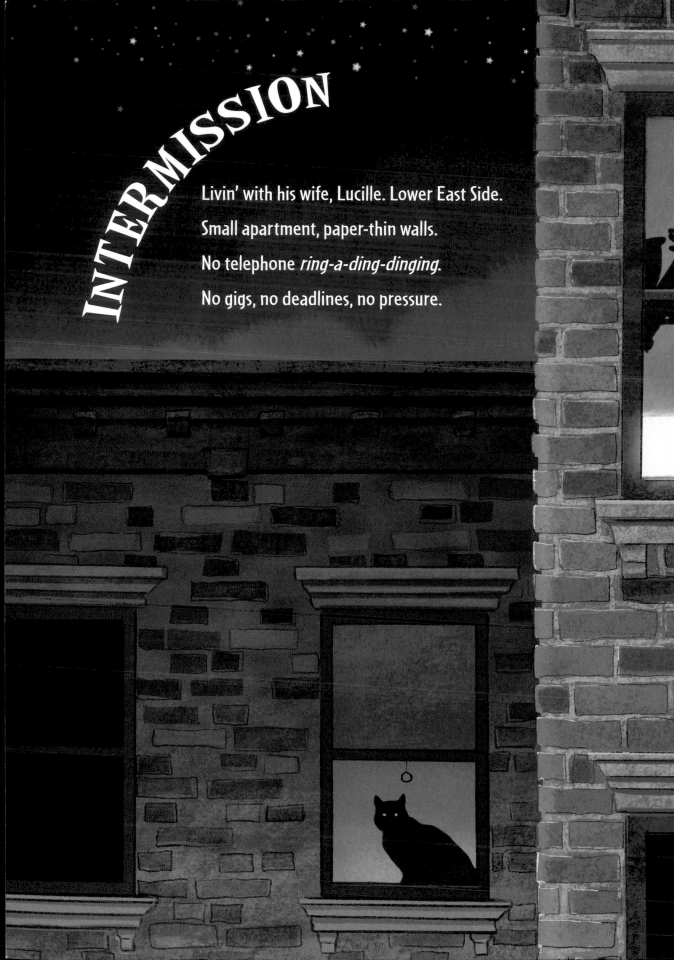

INTERMISSION

Livin' with his wife, Lucille. Lower East Side.

Small apartment, paper-thin walls.

No telephone *ring-a-ding-dinging.*

No gigs, no deadlines, no pressure.

Sixteen hours every day, plays to his heart's *de-light*.

Suits Sonny just fine

till a neighbor complains.

Hey, Sonny. I'm having a baby. Ain't nowhere else

you can blow that thing?

Puh-leeeeeeeeease?

Sorry, sorry, sorry, Sonny says.

Now Sonny's gotta find a place no one goes.

Where he can make notes cry and squeak, beg and plead,

bend 'em up, bend 'em sideways.

Where the heck in the Big Apple he's gonna find a place like *that*?

SECOND SET

Looks up—

That's it, Sonny says. *That's it!*

Hiding in plain sight.

The bridge named Williamsburg
connecting Manhattan to Brooklyn,
where he's gonna connect *the old* to *the new*—
from *what was* to what *will be*.
Isn't that what bridges do?

Sunrise, day. Sunset, night.

Neither rain nor snow nor heat nor cold

keeps Sonny away from his secret *ren-dez-vous*

with Henrietta.

(His beloved saxophone.)

Seeking refuge and *sol-i-tude*.

Finding inspiration, finding himself

in the echoes of the echoes of the echoes.

Trains clanking,

headlights flashing.

East River tugboats honking.

Sonny honks right back: *Take that, Jack!*

Up here, it hits you in the face.

So much sound, so much silence, so much space.

"This was heaven. This was *heaven*."

One year transposes into two.

HARD BEBOPPING NEWS DROPPING!

Excitement brewing like a steamy cup of joe at noon.

Sonny steps down from the bridge,

"'cause you can't be in heaven and on earth at the same time."

Rumors begin *per-co-lat-ing*.

Some say Sonny's found a new sound.

Some say he's not even playing sax anymore.

Some say Sonny's scared of the younger cats on the prowl.

Others sayin' Sonny's gonna *out-Sonny* Sonny.

New Sonny tunes it all out.

Glides back into the recording studio.

Dark shades on to keep the inside from getting out

and the outside from getting in.

Nods to the drummer, who starts the groove.

Stand-up bass follows, makes its move.

Electric guitar waits for a sign.

Sonny snappin' his fingers, lays down the melody in a

Nice. Straight. Line.

SONIC BEBOP BOOM BOOM BOP!

Sonny breaks the barrier,

enters a new dimension:

his subconscious

'cause "you can't think and play at the same time."

Two weeks. Winter 1962.

Three recording sessions and

Six. Tracks. Later.

That's it, Sonny beams. *That's it.*

Shiny vinyl-pressed hot wax.

The album titled

(drum roll, please)

The Bridge.

Now you know

all you gotta know

about the most humble, honest, and spiritual cat.

The one, the only, the legendary:

Mr. Walter Theodore "Sonny" Rollins.

Time Line

1930   Born September 7. Mother Valborg Rollins, from St. Thomas, works as a housekeeper. Father Walter Rollins, from St. Croix, is an officer in the US Navy.

1944   Mother buys him first saxophone. Gives him twenty-five cents a week for lessons.

1947   Graduates high school, joins musicians' union, gets first gigs.

1950   Arrested for armed robbery, sentenced to ten months at Rikers Island prison.

1951   Joins the Miles Davis Quintet. Makes first recordings as a band leader.

1955   Struggles with drug addiction. Lives on the streets in Chicago. Enters drug rehab. Works as a janitor in Chicago, begins playing sax again. Joins Clifford Brown & Max Roach Quintet.

1956   Records critically acclaimed LP *Saxophone Colossus*.

1957   Performs at Carnegie Hall.

1958   Records *Freedom Suite*, another landmark album. Appears in famous *A Great Day in Harlem* photograph.

1959–1961   Takes two-year sabbatical. Practices on pedestrian walkway on New York's Williamsburg Bridge. Studies music theory, begins a physical-fitness and healthy-eating regimen.

1962   Records *The Bridge* in two weeks in January and February.

1965   Marries Lucille Pearson.

1969–1971   Second sabbatical.

1972   Awarded a Guggenheim Fellowship.

1973   Elected as the 38th member of the *DownBeat* magazine Hall of Fame.

1981   Appears as uncredited guest soloist on the Rolling Stones' LP *Tattoo You*.

2002   Wins his first performance Grammy for *This Is What I Do* (2000).

2004   Receives a Lifetime Achievement Award from the National Academy of Recording Arts and Sciences.

2006   Wins second Grammy for "Why Was I Born," in the Best Jazz Instrumental Solo category (from the album *Without a Song: The 9/11 Concert*).

2008   Releases the first volume of *Road Shows*, a series of previously unreleased live performances.

2011   Receives the Medal of Arts from President Barack Obama in a White House ceremony. Accepts the award, the nation's highest honor for artistic excellence, and says he accepts "on behalf of the gods of our music."

2011   One of five 2011 Kennedy Center honorees. Sonny says, "In honoring me, the Kennedy Center honors jazz, America's classical music. For that, I am very grateful."

2012   Forced to end recording career and live performances because of physical requirements needed to play saxophone.

2015   *The Bridge* (1962) is inducted into the Grammy Hall of Fame.

2017   Campaign initiated by Lower East Side resident to rename the Williamsburg Bridge in Sonny's honor.

2017   *Saxophone Colossus* (1956) is named to the National Recording Registry of the Library of Congress.

2017   Donates archives to the Schomburg Center for Research in Black Culture, a research library of the New York Public Library and an archive repository for information on people of African descent worldwide.

2017   Honored with musical tribute at the 60th annual Monterey Jazz Festival.

2017   The Sonny Rollins Bridge Project is founded, seeking to rename the Williamsburg Bridge in Sonny's honor.

2018   Celebrates 88th birthday.

Sonny Quotes

Pg. 26: "This was heaven . . ." Chris Richards, "Sonny Rollins: A jazz mind in pursuit of improvisational heaven," *Washington Post*, December 12, 2011, www.washingtonpost.com/lifestyle/style/sonny-rollins-a-jazz-mind-in-pursuit-of-improvisational-heaven/2011/11/22/gIQA3aPsKO_story.html?utm_term.

Pg. 28: "Cause you can't be in heaven . . ." Sonny Rollins, "Sax and Sky," *New York Times Magazine*, April 23, 2015, www.nytimes.com/2015/04/26/magazine/sax-and-sky.html?ref=magazine.

Pg. 30: "You can't think . . ." Sonny Rollins, interviewed by Arun Rath, "Sonny Rollins: 'You Can't Think and Play at the Same Time,'" NPR Music: Music Interviews, May 3, 2014, www.npr.org/templates/transcript/transcript.php?storyId=309047616.

Learn More

Remember that you can always use your favorite internet search engine to find more about Sonny Rollins.

Web

Sonny Rollins's website.
www.sonnyrollins.com

The Schomburg Center for Research in Black Culture, which holds Sonny's personal archive.
www.nypl.org/locations/schomburg

Video

Burns, Ken, dir. *Jazz* (ten-part series). PBS, 2001.
www.pbs.org/kenburns/jazz/about

Fontaine, Dick, dir. *Sonny Rollins: Beyond the Notes*. BBC, 2014.
www.amazon.com/Sonny-Rollins-Beyond-Notes/dp/B0747V2PKN

———. Who Is? "Sonny Rollins with Paul Jeffrey." Allan King Associates Canada LTD, 1968. www.vimeo.com/5124602

Mugge, Robert, dir. *Saxophone Colossus* (Sonny Rollins concert documentary). MVD Visual, 1986. www.robertmugge.com/sonny-rollins/index.html

Picture Books

Orgill, Roxane. *Jazz Day: The Making of a Famous Photograph*. Somerville, MA: Candlewick Press, 2016.

Weatherford, Carole Boston and R. Gregory Christie. *Sugar Hill: Harlem's Historic Neighborhood*. Chicago: Albert Whitman & Company, 2014.

Selected Bibliography

Books

Blancq, Charles C. *Sonny Rollins: The Journey of a Jazzman*. Boston: Twayne, 1983.

Blumenthal, Bob, and John Abbott. *Saxophone Colossus: A Portrait of Sonny Rollins*. New York: Abrams, 2010.

Nisenson, Eric. *Open Sky: Sonny Rollins and His World of Improvisation*. New York: St. Martin's Press, 2000.

Web

Deluke, R.J. "Sonny Rollins: Still Seeking the Lost Chord." *All About Jazz*, January 13, 2009. www.allaboutjazz.com/sonny-rollins-still-seeking-the-lost-chord-sonny-rollins-by-rj-deluke.

Johnson, David. "Crossing the Bridge: The Return of Sonny Rollins." *Night Lights Classic Jazz*, Indiana Public Media, September 7, 2015. www.indianapublicmedia.org/nightlights/crossing-bridge-return-sonny-rollins.

McNally, Owen. "Sonny Rollins Reflects on His Life, Career, and Goals, Both Musical and Spiritual." WNPR News, May 20, 2015. www.wnpr.org/post/sonny-rollins-reflects-his-life-career-and-goals-both-musical-and-spiritual.

Redley, Simon. "WORLD EXCLUSIVE: Sonny Rollins: Horn Of Plenty (Part 1)." *Music Republic Magazine*, December 2016. www.musicrepublicmagazine.com/2016/12/sonny-rollins-horn-plenty-part-1.

Redman, Joshua. "Sonny Rollins Interviewed by Joshua Redman: Newk's Time." JazzTimes, June 1, 2005. www.jazztimes.com/features/sonny-rollins-interviewed-by-joshua-redman-newks-time.

For Mike Himelstein—B. W.

To my father, Boyd, who played a mean harmonica—K. M.

Special thanks to Yoron Israel, jazz drummer, bandleader, composer, and Berklee College of Music professor and co-chair of the percussion department, for reading the manuscript and providing valuable feedback. Mr. Israel has had the unique pleasure of touring and performing with Sonny Rollins.

Published by Charlesbridge
85 Main Street
Watertown, MA 02472
(617) 926-0329
www.charlesbridge.com

Illustrations created digitally using Procreate software
and Adobe Photoshop
Display type set in Crunchy Taco by Chris Garrett
Text type set in Cafeteria by The Font Bureau, Inc.
Color separations by Colourscan Print Co Pte Ltd, Singapore
Printed by 1010 Printing International Limited in
Huizhou, Guangdong, China
Production supervision by Brian G. Walker
Designed by Diane M. Earley

THE BRIDGE
Sonny Rollins

LSP 2527   SIDE 1
(N2PY-1268)

1 – WITHOUT A SONG
(Youmans-Rose-Eliscu)
2 – WHERE ARE YOU
(McHugh-Adamson)
3 – JOHN S.
(S. Rollins)

STEREO

**Library of Congress
Cataloging-in-Publication Data**
Names: Wittenstein, Barry, author. |
Mallett, Keith, illustrator.
Title: Sonny's bridge: jazz legend Sonny Rollins
finds his groove / Barry Wittenstein;
illustrated by Keith Mallett.
Description: Watertown, MA : Charlesbridge, 2019.
Identifiers: LCCN 2018014918 (print) |
LCCN 2018016093 (ebook) |
ISBN 9781632897381 (ebook) |
ISBN 9781632897398 (ebook pdf) |
ISBN 9781580898812 (reinforced for library use)
Subjects: LCSH: Rollins, Sonny—Juvenile literature. |
Jazz musicians—United States—Juvenile literature. |
Saxophonists—United States—Juvenile literature.
Classification: LCC ML3930.R645 (ebook) | LCC
ML3930.R645 W58 2019 (print) | DDC 788.7/165092
[B]—dc23
LC record available at
https://lccn.loc.gov/2018014918

Printed in China
(hc) 10 9 8 7 6 5 4 3 2 1